Saint Bernard
Mountain Rescuer

by Jessica Rudolph

Consultant: Karen Bodeving
President, Saint Bernard Club of America

New York, New York

Credits

Cover and Title Page, © Stockbrokerxtra Images/Photolibrary; TOC, © Jeannie Harrison/Close Encounters of the Furry Kind; 4, © Steve Loveless Photography, Beulah, MI; 5, © Steve Loveless Photography, Beulah, MI; 6, © Steve Loveless Photography, Beulah, MI; 7, © Paul Payne/Paul's Photography; 8, © Mary Evans Picture Library/Everett Collection; 9L, © Mary Evans Picture Library; 9R, © Mary Evans Picture Library; 10T, © Corbis/SuperStock; 10B, © Mary Evans Picture Library; 11L, © Mary Evans Picture Library; 11R, © Glenn Harper/Alamy; 12, © Yann Arthus-Bertrand/Corbis; 13L, © NaturePL/SuperStock; 13R, © Barbara O'Brien Photography; 14L, © Jeannie Harrison/Close Encounters of the Furry Kind; 14M, © Juniors Bildarchiv/Photolibrary; 14R, © Exactostock/SuperStock; 15T, © Animals Animals/SuperStock; 15B, © Karen Bodeving; 16L, © Sally Anne Thompson/Animal-Photography; 16R, © AP Photo/Keystone/Olivier Maire; 17, © Charles Thatcher/Stone/Getty Images; 18L, © Jim Holden/Alamy; 18R, © Nataliesusu/Dreamstime; 19, © Klein & Hubert/BIOS/Photolibrary; 20, © Jeannie Harrison/Close Encounters of the Furry Kind; 21L, © Jeannie Harrison/Close Encounters of the Furry Kind; 21R, © Glenn Kahl/Manteca Bulletin; 22, © Karen Bodeving; 23L, © Ronald Grant Archive/Mary Evans Picture Library/Everett Collection 23R, © Advertising Archive/Everett Collection; 24, © Dennis Bucklin; 25, © Dennis Bucklin; 26, © Jeannie Harrison/Close Encounters of the Furry Kind; 27, © Daniel Johnson/Fox Hill Photo; 28, © Malcolm S. Kirk/Peter Arnold/Photolibrary; 29T, © Eric Isselée/Shutterstock; 29B, © Karen Bodeving; 31, © Eric Isselée/Shutterstock; 32, © Michael Chen/iStockphoto.

Publisher: Kenn Goin
Senior Editor: Lisa Wiseman
Creative Director: Spencer Brinker
Design: Dawn Beard Creative
Cover Design: Dawn Beard Creative and Kim Jones
Photo Researcher: Mary Fran Loftus

Library of Congress Cataloging-in-Publication Data

Rudolph, Jessica.
 Saint Bernard : mountain rescuer / by Jessica Rudolph.
   p. cm. — (Big dogs rule)
 Includes bibliographical references and index.
 ISBN-13: 978-1-61772-295-0 (library binding)
 ISBN-10: 1-61772-295-2 (library binding)
 1. Saint Bernard dog—Juvenile literature. I. Title.
 SF429.S3R73 2012
 636.73—dc22
                          2011002431

For more information, write to Bearport Publishing Company, Inc., 45 West 21st Street, Suite 3B, New York, New York 10010. Printed in the United States of America in North Mankato, Minnesota.

070111
042711CGA

10 9 8 7 6 5 4 3 2 1

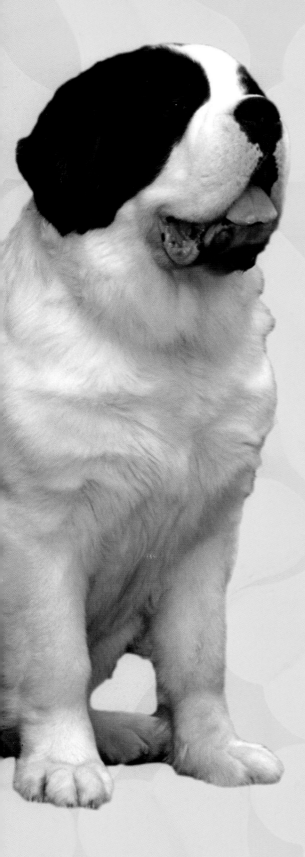

Contents

Katie Goes to Work

When kids go to the Interlochen Public Library in Michigan, they usually expect to find books, magazines, and DVDs. What they don't expect to find is Katie—a 130-pound (59-kg) Saint Bernard. Katie loves to give kisses and be petted. However, she has an important job to do at the library.

Katie visits the library once a month with her owner, Donald Williams.

Katie is a **therapy dog**. She works at the library encouraging children to read books. She also helps those who have trouble reading. To do this, Katie simply sits patiently by a child's side as he or she reads. Kids don't feel embarrassed if they make a mistake such as stumbling over a word. Katie doesn't laugh or make them feel bad. She just listens to them.

▲ **Katie listens to a child read at the Interlochen Public Library.**

Therapy dogs often visit patients in nursing homes and hospitals. Their job is to cheer up people. Some therapy dogs help people practice skills, such as throwing and catching a ball, that will make their bodies stronger.

A Good Listener

Janette Grice is the director of the Interlochen Public Library. She says Katie "helps kids feel comfortable and welcome when they come to the library." With a furry friend around, kids are able to relax and enjoy reading rather than fear it. Over time, they become better readers. Because of Katie's help, Janette says, "the kids just love her."

▲ **Katie, shown here with Janette Grice (left) and a young reader, likes to give lots of kisses to the children who read to her!**

The relationship Katie has with the children that come to the library is typical of a Saint Bernard. These dogs are known for being gentle, calm, and well behaved. While they have many good **traits**, perhaps their most important one is that they love helping people.

Katie is not the only dog that works at the Interlochen Public Library. She is sometimes joined by Denny, a Welsh Corgi that also listens to children read.

▲ **Katie and her pal, Denny, at the library**

Mountain Rescuer

Saint Bernards, or Saints, first started helping people in Switzerland hundreds of years ago. They pulled heavy dairy carts and worked as guard dogs for farmers. Then in the 1600s, these farm dogs began working with the **monks** who ran the Saint Bernard **Hospice**.

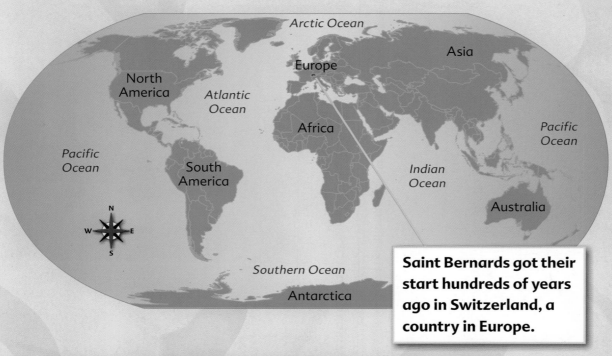

Saint Bernards got their start hundreds of years ago in Switzerland, a country in Europe.

◀ For hundreds of years, Swiss farmers used the strong Saint Bernards to pull carts filled with milk to be delivered to customers.

Located high in the mountains of Switzerland, the hospice is a safe place for people to rest as they travel over the dangerous Swiss Alps. The temperature in this area can dip to –20°F (–29°C). Mounds of snow can be 30 feet (9 m) deep. It's easy for people to get lost or buried in the snow and freeze to death. In the 1600s, after snowstorms or **avalanches**, the hospice monks would go out looking for the lost or injured. They took along the farm dogs to help them rescue these travelers.

▲ **This photo, from the 1930s, shows a monk and a Saint Bernard demonstrating how to rescue a traveler buried under snow.**

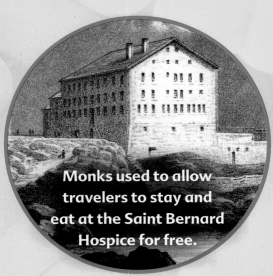

Monks used to allow travelers to stay and eat at the Saint Bernard Hospice for free.

Today, Saint Bernards still live with the monks at the hospice during certain times of the year. However, they are no longer used for rescue work.

Life Savers

Saint Bernards were perfectly suited for rescue work. Their thick fur kept them warm, allowing them to stay outside for hours without freezing. Their great sense of smell helped them locate lost or hurt travelers. Their huge, muscular bodies cleared paths in the deep snow when they walked, allowing the monks and travelers to easily follow behind them. The dogs could even sense when an avalanche was about to occur.

A Saint Bernard's thick fur helps it stay warm in cold weather more easily than some other types of dogs.

Artists used to show Saint Bernards ▶ with small barrels, filled with a type of alcohol called brandy, tied around their necks. People used to think brandy would warm up travelers lost in the snow. The monks, however, say that the dogs never carried the barrels on rescues.

Sometimes small groups of dogs went on rescue **missions** without human help. If the dogs found a person buried under snow, they dug the traveler out with their massive paws. Then one dog would lie on top of the person to keep him or her warm. The other dogs would race back to the hospice to get help. In over 200 years, the Saint Bernards saved more than 2,000 people.

◀ **Saint Bernards can smell a person up to 2 miles (3.2 km) away and find someone buried under 14 feet (4.3 m) of snow!**

Saint Bernards got their name in the 1880s. Before then, they were known by many different names such as Hospice dogs, Saint Bernard Mastiffs, Mountain dogs, and Swiss Alpine dogs.

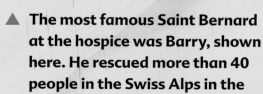

▲ **The most famous Saint Bernard at the hospice was Barry, shown here. He rescued more than 40 people in the Swiss Alps in the early 1800s.**

Giant Pets

Today's Saint Bernards are different than their **ancestors** in many ways. For example, these dogs no longer perform rescue work in the Swiss Alps. Instead, they have become lovable family pets. Modern-day Saint Bernards also look different than the old mountain rescuers. They have wider heads and shorter **muzzles**. They're also bigger. In fact, they're enormous!

A Saint's head can be as big as a basketball!

Saint Bernards are one of the largest of all dog **breeds**. On average, adult male Saints are about 30 inches (76 cm) tall at the shoulder and typically weigh between 160 and 180 pounds (73 and 82 kg). That's about the same weight as an average human adult male.

As rescue dogs, Saints used their large size to help them clear paths in snowy weather. As pets, however, their big size can sometimes get these lovable giants into trouble. For example, they're tall enough to grab food off counters. If they're not careful, a flick of their tails can easily knock plates off a table. Saint Bernard owners need to keep a careful eye on their pets to make sure they stay out of trouble.

▲ **When standing on two legs, Saint Bernards can be as tall as their owners.**

◀ **Saint Bernards can easily get to food left out on counters and tables.**

Saint Bernards became popular in the 1800s when people around the world learned about the heroic dogs of the Saint Bernard Hospice. Saints were first brought to the United States as pets in the 1880s.

The Long and Short of It

Saint Bernards have one of two kinds of **coats**—longhaired or shorthaired. Hundreds of years ago, all Saints were shorthaired. In 1830, the Swiss monks **bred** their dogs with Newfoundlands, a dog breed with long hair. They hoped longer hair would keep the dogs warmer in harsh weather.

Unfortunately, when out in the cold searching for travelers, clumps of ice formed on the longhaired Saint's fluffy fur. The extra weight from the ice slowed them down. So the monks gave away the longhaired dogs to farmers and went back to breeding only shorthaired dogs for rescue work.

▲ **Shorthaired Saint Bernards (left) were bred with Newfoundlands (middle) to create longhaired Saint Bernards (right) with long, silky fur.**

Both types of Saints still exist today, however. Whether long or shorthaired, Saints can have the same coat colors and markings. Most have some white fur on their chests, necks, feet, tails, and muzzles. Colored patches of fur on their bodies can be several shades of red or brown. Dark fur around the eyes and ears creates a "mask" on many Saints.

◄ **This Saint Bernard has a half mask. That means it has dark-colored fur around only one eye.**

The Swiss monks first got the idea to breed longhaired Saint Bernards after many of their shorthaired dogs died while doing rescue work during extremely cold winters in the early 1800s.

▲ **This Saint Bernard has a hospice ear, which means his ear has some white fur on it.**

Loving and Lazy

Saint Bernards make great family pets for many reasons. They're sweet, affectionate, and love to be around people. When their families come home, Saints like to greet them with slobbery kisses.

Saint Bernards are very **tolerant** of children, too. They seem to enjoy hugs from kids. They're patient even if a child accidentally steps on a paw or pulls their fur.

Saint Bernards love to give kisses.

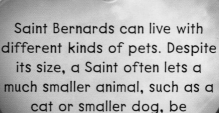

Saint Bernards can live with different kinds of pets. Despite its size, a Saint often lets a much smaller animal, such as a cat or smaller dog, be the boss of the house.

Saints are also known for being laid-back. Although very playful as puppies, adults are less active. Sleeping is one of their favorite activities. Unless **trained** not to, Saint Bernards will take naps on beds and sofas. They often seek out a person to snuggle with at bedtime.

▲ **Saints prefer to nap with a pal.**

Fast-Growing Puppies

It's hard to believe, but Saint Bernards start out very small. At birth, they weigh just over one pound (.5 kg). At first the puppies are helpless. Their eyes are closed, and they can only crawl. They spend their days sleeping and drinking milk from their mother's body. Within a few weeks, though, the puppies in a **litter** gain enough strength to start jumping and playing with one another.

Saint Bernard puppies grow quickly. ▶
However, it can take up to three years
for them to reach full size.

When they're first born, longhaired Saint Bernard puppies look just like the shorthaired puppies. It can take up to six weeks for the longhaired puppies' fur to grow out and fluff up.

▲ **Saint litters are large—usually**
made up of about 8 to 10 puppies.
This litter has 13 pups!

Saint pups grow quickly. By eight weeks, they're already about 15 to 20 pounds (6.8 to 9 kg). That's the size of a full-grown cocker spaniel dog. At this age, the puppies are ready to become part of a human family.

▲ **Eight-week-old pups with their mother**

Quick Learners

Training is a must for Saint Bernard puppies as soon as they're brought to their new homes. Without it, the adorable balls of fur soon become huge and hard to control. A six-month-old puppy with no training is so big that it could easily knock someone down. Luckily, Saints are very smart and eager to please. They can quickly learn to not jump on people and to walk on a leash without pulling.

▲ **If Saints aren't trained, they could be the ones taking their owners for a walk.**

To begin their training, owners should teach their dogs commands such as "sit" and "come." Saints are sensitive, though. Their feelings can get hurt if they're yelled at. So owners should speak gently to their pets and use treats or **praise** during training.

Owners should also get their pets used to seeing and hearing new things, such as cars. By doing this, their dogs will quickly learn to adjust to new experiences.

▲ **Hercules**

▲ **Saints are sometimes a little slow to follow a command they know, such as "sit." This doesn't mean they're not smart. They just need a bit more time to move their large bodies.**

A Saint Bernard in California named Hercules was taught to fetch the newspaper in the morning for his owner. However, Hercules learned too well. He not only got his owner's paper but started fetching all the neighbors' newspapers, too!

Working Hard

Saint Bernards can learn a lot more than simple commands. Some are taught to pull carts just like their ancestors used to do in Switzerland. These Saints show off their skills in **drafting competitions**.

During these events, Saint Bernards pull heavy carts while following commands. The dogs have to stop, change speed, and make sharp turns without letting the cart fall over. Only the steadiest dogs win.

Some Saints compete in weight-pulling competitions. In these events, the dogs pull carts on wheels or snow sleds that are weighted down. More and more weight is added until the dogs can no longer pull the carts or sleds.

A Saint Bernard competing in a drafting event

While some Saint Bernards compete in drafting competitions, others are used in **advertisements** to help sell products such as cereal, oranges, and chocolate. Still other Saint Bernards star in movies. *Beethoven*, a film that was made in 1992, is one of the most well-known movies featuring this giant breed. It is about a destructive but lovable Saint Bernard and his family.

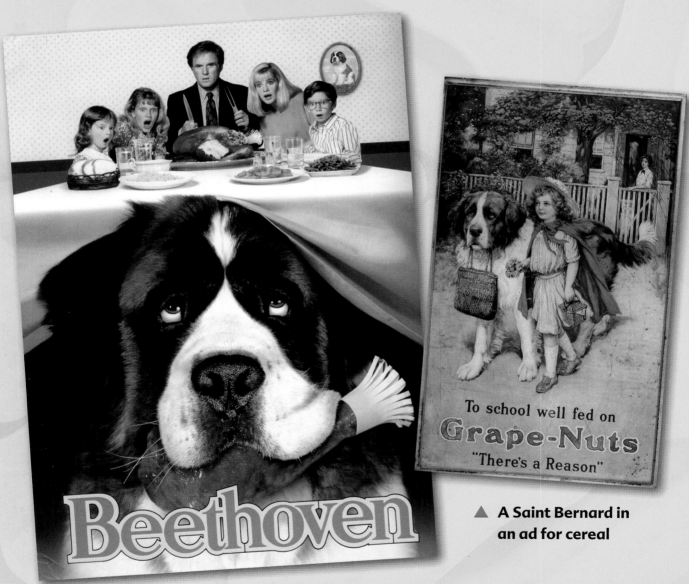

▲ A poster from the movie *Beethoven*

▲ A Saint Bernard in an ad for cereal

Still Helping People

Katie, the Saint Bernard from the Interlochen Public Library, is not the only big dog that likes working with children. Penny is another Saint Bernard that spends her time helping the young. Penny works as a **service dog** for Nathan, a boy with **autism**.

▲ **Nathan with his mom and Penny**

Sometimes Nathan can get into unsafe situations. For instance, he might try to run away from his mother into a busy street. However, Penny is there to keep Nathan safe. She's attached to him with a **harness**. If Nathan tries to run away, Penny stays very still and keeps Nathan from moving. She stays this way until Nathan has calmed down.

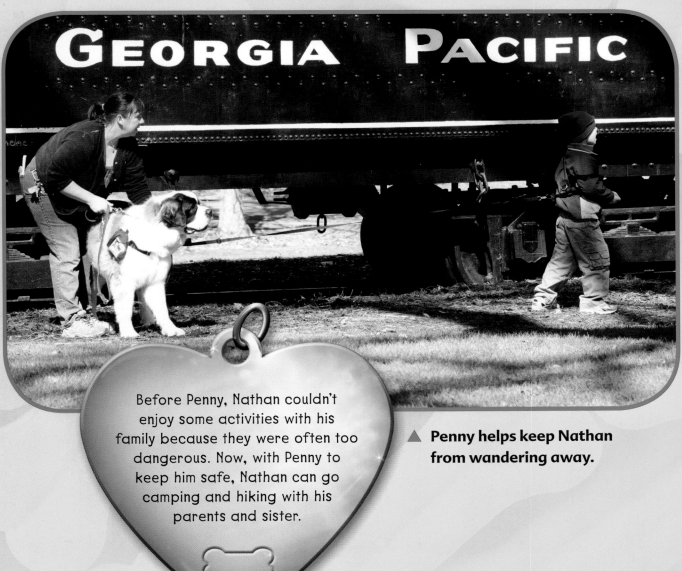

Before Penny, Nathan couldn't enjoy some activities with his family because they were often too dangerous. Now, with Penny to keep him safe, Nathan can go camping and hiking with his parents and sister.

▲ **Penny helps keep Nathan from wandering away.**

Big Responsibilities, Big Rewards

A person who is thinking about getting a Saint as a pet should know that a big dog is a big responsibility. Saint Bernards eat a lot of food. As a result, they need to be taken outside often so they can go to the bathroom. They drool and **shed** more than some other dog breeds, too. So owners need to clean up after them more than they would with other types of dogs. Daily exercise and lots of attention are also needed to keep Saints healthy and happy.

Saint Bernards usually live eight to ten years. Those that are fed well, exercised daily, and taken to the **veterinarian** regularly may live even longer.

▲ **Owners need to brush their dogs' hair every day. Most Saints look forward to this daily brushing.**

For people who want to take on these responsibilities, Saint Bernards offer big rewards. Their size and sweet expressions attract attention wherever they go. At home, they're loyal, caring, and good-natured. For the right person, a Saint Bernard can provide years of loving friendship.

Saint Bernards at a Glance

Weight:	Males: 160–180 pounds (73–82 kg) Females: 110–150 pounds (50–68 kg)
Height at Shoulder:	Males: 29–32 inches (74–81 cm) Females: 26–29 inches (66–74 cm)
Coat Hair:	Short, thick, and smooth; or long hair that's straight or wavy
Colors:	White with different shades of red or brown
Country of Origin:	Switzerland
Life Span:	About 8–10 years
Personality:	Gentle, friendly, playful; calm, even under stress; eager to please; enjoys the company of people and other animals

Best in Show

What makes a great Saint Bernard? Every owner knows that his or her dog is special. Judges in dog shows, however, look very carefully at a Saint Bernard's appearance and behavior. Here are some of the things they look for:

dark brown eyes with an intelligent and friendly expression

large, wide head, slightly curved on top

broad, black nose with wide, open nostrils

Behavior: calm, gentle, friendly

ears set high with a rounded, triangular shape

long, heavy tail that hangs straight down, sometimes slightly curved at the end

short and straight muzzle

long or short coat; white markings on the chest, feet, tip of tail, muzzle, and neck, with colored patches that can be red or brown; never one color or without white

powerful, muscular body and legs

large, round feet with high-set knuckles and thick pads

Glossary

advertisements (AD-vur-*tize*-muhnts) announcements in newspapers or magazines, or on radio or television, that call attention to things such as products or events

ancestors (AN-sess-turz) family members who lived a long time ago

autism (AW-tiz-uhm) a condition that causes people to have trouble communicating with and relating to others

avalanches (AV-uh-*lanch*-iz) large amounts of snow, ice, or earth that suddenly move down a mountain at a fast speed without warning

bred (BRED) when dogs from specific breeds are mated to produce young with certain characteristics

breeds (BREEDZ) kinds of dogs

coats (KOHTS) the fur or hair on dogs or other animals

drafting competitions (DRAF-ting *kom*-puh-TISH-uhnz) contests in which dogs pull weighted carts and follow commands

harness (HAR-niss) a device attached to an animal that allows a person to hold on to the animal

hospice (HOSS-piss) an inn for travelers that is run by a religious community

litter (LIT-ur) a group of baby animals that are born to the same mother at the same time

missions (MISH-uhnz) important jobs or tasks

monks (MUHNGKS) religious men who have devoted their lives to prayer and teaching

muzzles (MUH-zuhlz) the noses, mouths, and jaws of some kinds of animals, such as dogs

praise (PRAYZ) enthusiastic words of approval

service dog (SUR-viss DAWG) a dog that is trained to do tasks for people who have disabilities or health problems

shed (SHED) to have fur or hair fall off a body

therapy dog (THER-uh-pee DAWG) a dog that visits hospitals and other places to cheer up people and make them feel more comfortable

tolerant (TOL-ur-uhnt) to put up with something harmful or unpleasant

trained (TRAYND) taught to do certain things

traits (TRAYTS) qualities or characteristics of people or animals

veterinarian (*vet*-ur-uh-NER-ee-uhn) a doctor who takes care of dogs and other animals

Bibliography

Walker, Joan Hustace. *Saint Bernards: A Complete Pet Owner's Manual.* Hauppauge, NY: Barron's Educational Series (1998).

www.akc.org/breeds/saint_bernard/

www.saintbernardclub.org

Read More

Hall, Lynn. *Barry: The Bravest Saint Bernard.* New York: Random House (2007).

Landau, Elaine. *Saint Bernards are the Best.* Minneapolis, MN: Lerner Publishing Group (2011).

Wilcox, Charlotte. *The Saint Bernard.* Mankato, MN: Capstone Press (1998).

Learn More Online

To learn more about Saint Bernards, visit
www.bearportpublishing.com/BigDogsRule

Index

About the Author

Jessica Rudolph has edited many books about animals.
She lives in Arizona with a big dog—a Great Dane named Boris.